Fit Can Be Fun!

A Kid's Guide to Healthy Choices

Written by J.S. Jackson
Illustrated by R.W. Alley

ONE
CARING
PLACE

Abbey Press
St. Meinrad, IN 47577

I am dedicating this book to all of you wonderful kids out there who are struggling with your weight and fitness. I know you all have a wonderful, loving nature, a good sense of humor, and you are doing the best you can. I know this because I am one of you. I wish you luck and success. Remember, you CAN do it!

Text © 2011 J.S. Jackson
Illustrations © 2011 Saint Meinrad Archabbey
Published by One Caring Place
Abbey Press
St. Meinrad, Indiana 47577

Library of Congress Catalog Number
2010915191

ISBN 978-0-87029-453-2

Printed in the United States of America

A Message to Parents, Teachers, and Other Caring Adults

As parents, we have all heard the term "Obesity Epidemic," especially as it pertains to our young ones. Statistics show that about 33% of the US population is obese… and 67% is overweight.

There are many reasons for this. In today's economy, both parents now work in over 75% of families. This means there is less time for healthy food shopping and preparation. We often find ourselves relying on fast food outlets and their predominance of high-fat, high-sugar food.

Another culprit is the television set (and often the video games that go with it). TV watching and game playing should be limited to 1-2 hours per day. The rest of the time can be spent reading, doing homework, or having fun playing with friends outdoors. In bad weather, indoor activities such as dancing, hula hoop, or jump rope are great.

One of the things kids get teased about most is their body shape. Overweight kids—even slightly overweight—are often teased quite mercilessly. This can be very devastating. If this is occurring, our kids need all the understanding and support we can give them. Suggest "turning over a new leaf" with healthy eating and regular exercise ("play") for everyone. Show them how much fun it is to feel fit.

Having family dinner at home can be a great experience for everybody. Studies show that in families where this is done, kids are less likely to become obese. It's also a great opportunity to build family togetherness. When possible, a regular family walk after dinner can do wonders. And don't forget to stock up on fresh fruits and other healthy snacks.

Always remember, children mirror their parent's actions. The best thing we can do for our kids is to set a good example by eating healthy and exercising. The more we can share this together, the better off we'll all be. We'll have families that know it's fun to be fit!

—*J.S. Jackson*

It's Fun to Be Fit

People come in all shapes and sizes. That's the way God makes us. How boring would it be if we all looked the same!

Some things we can't change, like how tall we are or the color of our eyes. Some things we can, like how we treat other people or how we take care of our bodies. This book is about taking care of our bodies so they work the best they can. You'll find that life is a lot more fun when you have a body that works well.

Reasons to Be Fit

Whether you're running around a field or running around with friends, nobody wants to be running last. You get sweaty and out of breath and have to sit down and rest before others.

When you're fit, you'll have more energy to do more things. Your body will work better and even your brain will work better. When you're clothes shopping, it's a great feeling to be able to buy and wear the same sizes as other kids your age. You might even get compliments on how nice you look in your new shirt or jeans.

Food Is Fuel to Make Your Body Work

Everyone has to eat to live. Food gives us the energy and strength we need for our bodies and our minds. There are different types of foods we need to eat in order to get the winning combination that works best for us.

The right combinations will help us to run faster, jump higher, play longer… and even think more clearly. The wrong combinations slow us down, make us tired faster, and cause us to gain more weight than is healthy.

On the next page you'll go to the "Elf-Healthy Fun Food Picnic," where you'll find the foods you can choose for making healthy combinations.

Eating Out

Some people call fast food "fat food" as a joke. Sure, some of the choices are high in fat, but if you're smart, you can get a tasty meal that's healthy, too!

Most fast food restaurants will give you or your parents a Nutrition Guide for their foods. Then you can play a fun game with your parents of building the tastiest meal using the healthiest ingredients.

If you use the "drive thru," wait until you get home to eat and put the food out at the table so it feels like a real meal. Eating in front of the TV is a bad habit and you sometimes don't pay enough attention to what you're eating.

Eating at Home

Eating at home is usually a healthier option for mealtime, because there are so many things to choose from. It's like having the foods from the "Elf-Healthy Fun Food Picnic" in your kitchen. Try helping your parent put together an awesome meal!

When families have dinner together, it's one of the best things they can do! It gives them the chance to say grace and to talk about their days—*"How was work today?" "How was school today?" "What's the best thing that happened?" "What's the worst thing that happened?"* It's also a good time to plan weekend activities and trips.

Families that do this become closer and stronger… and have more fun!

After School Snacks

Afternoons can be a hard time for kids. You're home from school; you made it through another day. You haven't eaten for a while; maybe it's time for a little celebration. With dinner coming soon, it's a good time for a delicious, healthy snack.

Ask your parents to keep fruit in the fridge. You can choose from apples, oranges, bananas, grapes, strawberries, or watermelon.

Some people like to create little fun snacks like "Ants on a Log." Take a stick of celery and spread a little peanut butter down the middle. Then put raisins on the peanut butter and bam, you've got Ants on a Log!

Play Is Fun, Exercise Is Work!

What kids call "play," grown-ups might call "exercise." They're pretty much the same thing. We walk around or run around or play games like tag or tennis. We move our bodies a lot and we use up the "fuel" we put in them when we eat food. By doing that, we get more energy.

Kids are lucky because they're born to be active and play outdoors. This is the best thing in the world for keeping fit. But today there are a lot of other temptations, like TV, video games, and computers that keep them from getting enough exercise.

A good idea is to limit yourself to *"an-hour-a-day of sit-down play."*

The Great Outdoors

Whether it's hot or cold or sunny or cloudy, nothing beats how great playing outdoors makes you feel. There's something special about being in the fresh air and having the freedom to do what you want. It's one of life's most special feelings.

Kids are so good at outdoor games, you often just make up your own. Some of the more popular ones are: Hide 'n Seek, Tag, Simon Says, Monkey in the Middle, and Capture the Flag.

These fun games can be played for hours and you almost don't realize you're becoming healthier and happier.

The Great Indoors

When it's too cold or rainy outside, there's still a way to have some fun activities indoors.

One of the best ways to have indoor fun is to put on some of your favorite fast music and dance to it.

Keep a jump rope in your room and see how many times in a row you can skip over it. See if you can set a world record with a hula hoop.

If you have a little spongy ball, you can create almost any outdoor game and bring it inside. Spongy ball tennis, spongy ball volleyball, spongy ball ping pong… or make up a game of your own and give it a silly name.

Dealing with Feelings

If you are overweight or heading in that direction, you probably already know that there are a lot of feelings that come along with it. Sometimes, when you're feeling bad, having something to eat makes you feel better. That's just normal; everybody's like that. But if you're feeling bad about being overweight, then eating is probably the wrong thing to do.

One of the best things to do, luckily, is to do what you do best. Play. The exercise will help burn off that extra "fuel" you've been adding from foods and make you feel happier and healthier at the same time.

Teasing

Have other kids teased you about being overweight? If not, you're very lucky. Being overweight is one of the most common things kids get teased about. And it hurts. The words people use hurt and it hurts more when others laugh. You don't even have to be very much overweight. That teaser just likes to pick on people because he or she is a bully.

The best way to deal with any bully is not to show that it's getting to you. Act like you don't hear it. Or smile and say something like, "Thanks for noticing, I'm working on it."

Deciding to Do Something

Deciding to take action and do something about being overweight is a hard step to take. The first thing to do is try to get an adult to help support you with it, to guide you and encourage you. This could be a parent, a teacher, a nurse, a doctor, or a person in your church.

Anyone you ask will see how brave a step this is and will be happy to help you if they can. This can be the beginning of a wonderful journey.

God Always Loves You the Way You Are

There are all kinds of people in the world: short ones, tall ones, chubby ones, skinny ones. It's important to remember that God loves us all and wants the best for us. Asking God to help you could make a huge difference. God wants you to have a healthier, happier life.

Make God your "silent partner." In the morning, ask God to help you make wise food choices during the day. Before meals, ask God to help you eat what's best for your body. And at night, thank God for the help you have received. You'll be amazed what you can do.

J. S. Jackson is a husband, dad, and writer living in Lenexa, Kansas. The former manager of Hallmark Cards' creative writing staff, he is now a freelance writer and editor. A multi-tasking "Mr. Mom," he creates cards, books, and other inspirational materials from his messy home office.

R. W. Alley is the illustrator for the popular Abbey Press adult series of Elf-help books, as well as an illustrator and writer of children's books. He lives in Barrington, Rhode Island, with his wife, daughter, and son. See a wide variety of his works at: www.rwalley.com.